Pushing and pulling
Contents

Teacher's notes	1	See-saw	19
Push or pull?	5	Make a puppet	20
Pushes and pulls in the classroom	6	Lifting things	21
Changing shapes	7	Making things turn	22
Stretch and twist	8	Cogs and gears	23
Moving things	9	How things fall	24
Make it move!	10	How hard does it fall?	25
Rolling things	11	Will it bounce?	26
Wheels	12	Sink or float?	27
Make a buggy	13	Does shape affect floating?	28
Using ramps	14	Feeling the 'push' of water	29
Friction	15	Is salty water best for floating?	30
Pendulums	16	Water safety	31
Levers – 1	17	Balloon power	32
Levers – 2	18		

Teacher's notes

Aims of this book

- To provide opportunities for the children to explore the properties of forces; how they push, pull, make things move, stop and change the shape of objects.
- to provide experience in observing, predicting, recording, measuring and making hypotheses.
- to provide opportunities for children to share their ideas with others.

Developing science skills

While it is not essential to follow the order of the worksheets in this book, it is important that all those covering one aspect of a subject are dealt with at approximately the same time.

Although it is in the *doing* of science that children learn best, this involves more than just practical work. As well as needing to observe, record, predict, measure, look for patterns, classify, explain and ask questions that can lead to further investigations children need time to discuss their work, before and after the activity. This will help to monitor progress so that they build a valid framework for future development.

Scientific background

This information aims to help you to understand the scientific concepts and ideas covered in this book. It generally goes beyond the level of understanding expected of most children, but will give you the confidence to ask and answer questions and to guide the children in their investigations.

Forces affect the way things move, change the shape of an object and make it move slower or faster. Pushing, pulling, stretching, twisting, lifting and spinning are all forces.

Objects cannot move by themselves. They need a force to push or pull them. It takes more force to make things start to move or stop than it does to keep them moving.

Forces can occur naturally, such as gravity, wind and waves. Other forces can be produced by people or machines, such as pulling a string on a kite or the use of levers, pulleys and wheels.

Gravity

Gravity is the force which pulls objects to the ground. All objects have an invisible force which attracts them together. Large objects, such as the Earth, have strong powers of attraction, so smaller objects are pulled towards them; thus objects fall towards the Earth. As things fall, they accelerate. Objects that fall from a great height travel faster than ones that have fallen less far.

Air exerts friction on objects as they move through it. This is called *resistance* or *drag*. The amount of drag depends on the shape of the object. A piece of paper will fall slowly as the resistance acts against gravity, while a round object will fall quickly as it has less resistance.

Levers

A lever is a simple machine. Levers can be used to lift heavy or large objects more easily. They work best when the fulcrum is close to the object and the pushing point is as far away as possible.

Friction

When two objects rub together friction acts upon them. If the objects are rough or uneven, movement is more difficult. Friction can be helpful, for example the friction caused by the uneven soles of trainers help prevent us slipping.

Pendulums

Galileo discovered that the length of string affects how long a pendulum takes to swing, not the size of the 'bob' or weight on the end.

Floating and sinking

An object placed in water will displace water to make room for itself. If the mass of the water displaced by the object equals the mass of the object, the object will float. If the object's mass is greater than the mass of the water it displaces, the object sinks.

Density is a term used to compare the mass of the same volume of different substances. Salty water is denser than fresh water, therefore objects will float higher in salty water than fresh.

Notes on individual activities

Page 5: Push or pull

Key idea: things can be made to work by pushing or pulling them.
Likely outcome: by comparing results, children may find that some objects can be pushed and pulled, for example, a shopping trolley.
Extension: make a collection of objects or pictures of objects which can be pushed or pulled – use the collection to investigate further.

Page 6: Pushes and pulls in the classroom

Key idea: to see whether classroom objects have to be pushed or pulled to make them work.
Likely outcome: children may disagree about whether an object is pushed or pulled, or both, to make it work. This should lead to a very useful discussion about how things work/move.
Extension: look at objects in the home.

Page 7: Changing shapes

Key idea: to investigate how objects can change shape.
Likely outcome: some objects can change shape in a variety of ways; for example Plasticine can be rolled into a sausage shape or a ball, flattened, made into a cube, twisted and so on.
Extension: explore different ways of changing the shape of objects.

Page 8: Stretch and twist

Key idea: to investigate stretching and twisting to change the shape of objects.
Likely outcome: some objects can be twisted and stretched, although stretchy objects usually revert back to their original shape (elasticity).
Extension: explore other ways of changing objects, such as bending and squeezing.

Page 9: Moving things

Key idea: to explore how objects can be moved more easily – the use of rollers.
Likely outcome: rolling is easier than sliding. The string makes pulling easier.
Extension: try moving a heavy object, such as a large box, using rollers.

Page 10: Make it move!

Key idea: that objects have wheels, handles, pulleys and so on to make movement easier.
Likely outcome: movement is made easier by using wheels, cogs, pivots, springs and strings.
Extension: take apart toys and other objects to find out how they work.

Page 11: Rolling things

Key idea: to investigate what affects an object's ability to roll.
Likely outcome: round objects roll more easily. Rolling is affected by the object's weight, texture (which may affect friction) and shape.
Extension: try rolling the same objects on different surfaces – introduce the idea of friction.

Page 12: Wheels

Key idea: to make some wheels and investigate how they move.
Likely outcome: the plastic wheels are more rigid than the card ones and will work better. The surface will affect how well the wheels move. The investigation of slopes will introduce speed.
Extension: make wheels using other objects. Which wheels, axles and fixing methods are best?

Page 13: Make a buggy

Key idea: to make a vehicle that moves.
Likely outcome: the holes for the axles must be the right height to ensure that the wheels touch the ground.
Extension: make a buggy which moves using a battery and a small motor.
Safety precaution: children will need help to make holes in the ice-cream container.

Page 14: Using ramps

Key idea: to investigate the effect of a slope on speed and distance travelled.
Likely outcome: the greater the slope the further the car will travel because the speed is greater.
Extension: discuss the fact that the faster a vehicle moves, the harder it is to stop and the more damage or injury it causes if it hits anything.

Page 15: Friction
Key idea: to explore the effect of friction upon the movement of objects.
Likely outcome: the eraser will move more freely on smooth surfaces because these offer less resistance (friction).
Extension: investigate shoe soles.

Page 16: Pendulums
Key idea: to investigate what effects how an object swings.
Likely outcome: the pendulums will take the same amount of time to make ten swings, no matter how large the blob on the end. A short length of string will swing more quickly than a longer piece. It is the length of the string which affects how a pendulum swings.
Extension: make pendulums of gradually decreasing lengths. Graph the time taken to swing ten times for each length.

Page 17: Levers – 1
Key idea: to investigate how levers make things easier to move.
Likely outcome: the lid and nail will most likely not be moved by hand; the lever will make lifting easier. Holding the lever close to the end makes it most efficient.
Extension: explore how large and small scissors, pliers and shears work. Is there a relationship between the length of the cutting edge and the length of the handles from the fulcrum?
Safety precaution: care needs to be taken when hammering nails.

Page 18: Levers – 2
Key idea: to investigate the efficiency of levers.
Likely outcome: when the fulcrum (pivot) is in the middle, the further away from the fulcrum the pushing force is applied, the more efficient the lever becomes. When the fulcrum is closer to the end where the pushing force is applied, the less effort is needed to lift the load.
Extension: explore lifting heavy loads using levers, such as a plank of wood, to move a heavy box.

Page 19: See-saw
Key idea: to investigate how the distance from the fulcrum affects the balance of objects on a lever.
Likely outcome: the coins balance because the centre of gravity is in the middle. Work = force x distance, therefore two coins placed 2cm from the fulcrum will balance one coin placed 4cm from the fulcrum.
Extension: continue the investigation using more coins. Where do you have to put one coin to balance three, four and then five coins?

Page 20: Make a puppet
Key idea: to reinforce the notion of how levers work from a pivot.
Extension: the puppet's arms and legs could be made to move independently by using string.

Page 21: Lifting things
Key idea: to investigate how pulleys lift things.
Likely outcome: the bucket will lift much more easily with the pulley.
Extension: make pulleys using two or more reels and more string.

Page 22: Making things turn
Key idea: to investigate how turning one object can turn another.
Likely outcome:

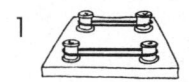

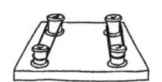

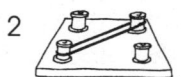

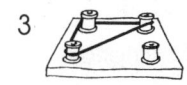

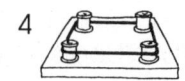

Extension: make a vehicle such as a tank.
Safety precautions: care needs to be taken when hammering nails.

Page 23: Cogs and gears
Key idea: to investigate how gears work.
Likely outcome: the smaller cog will turn more often than the large one and will turn in the opposite direction.
Extension: look at gears in a bicycle.
Safety precautions: children will need help when piercing holes in the boxes.

Page 24: How things fall
Key idea: to explore gravity.
Likely outcome: objects of the same size and shape fall at the same speed even if they do not weigh the same. The paper will flutter to the floor as its shape offers more resistance in the air.
Extension: make a parachute to demonstrate the idea of resistance.

Page 25: How hard does it fall?
Key idea: to find out if height affects how hard an object hits the ground when it falls.
Likely outcome: objects falling from a greater height travel faster than those falling from a lower height. They will make a bigger dent in the clay.
Extension: investigate whether pushing an object makes it fall faster than just dropping it.

Page 26: Will it bounce?
Key ideas: to investigate factors which affect

whether an object will bounce or not and how high it will bounce.
Likely outcome: a ball bounces because as it hits the ground it squashes out of shape; as it springs back into shape it pushes itself off the ground.
Extension: how far can the objects be thrown.

Page 27: Sink or float?
Key idea: to see if objects will float or sink.
Likely outcome: floaters – bean, plastic ruler (if placed flat), most kinds of wood and the foil tray. The wooden peg will float at first but may sink due to the metal clip. The jar may float depending on how it is placed in the water. The only wood which will sink is *Lignum vitae*.
Extension: make the floaters sink.

Page 28: Does shape affect floating?
Key idea: to investigate how shape affects whether an object sinks or floats.
Likely outcome: the Plasticine will float if made into a shape with a large surface area. The sides of the boat will need to be quite high and all corners sealed before it will float.
Extension: make boats from different materials.

Page 29: Feeling the 'push' of water:
Key idea: to investigate buoyancy.
Likely outcome: the ping-pong ball will sink if it is pushed because the hand increases its mass. When released, the force of buoyancy causes the ball to rise up quickly. The balls will float lower in the water with each increasing weight until the mass is greater than the amount of water displaced and the ball sinks.
Extension: make an object that sinks and floats.

Page 30: Is salty water best for floating?
Key idea: to investigate how objects float in fresh and salty water.
Likely outcome: the boat will float higher in the salty water because salty water is more dense than tap water. The boat will thus hold more counters in salty water before it sinks.
Extension: investigate how different water temperatures affect floating.

Page 31: Water safety
Key idea: to reinforce knowledge about objects that will float.
Likely outcome: floaters – rubber ring, arm bands, beach ball, wood.
Extension: discuss other aspects of water safety.

Page 32: Balloon power
Key idea: to investigate the pushing effect of air being released.
Likely outcome: as the air is released the boat will be pushed forward.
Extension: explore other sources of power.

National Curriculum: Science
In addition to the PoS for AT1, the following PoS are relevant to this book:
AT4 – Pupils should: • have early experience of devices which move. They should experience the natural force of gravity pulling things down and manufactured forces. These forces should be experienced in the way they push, pull, make things move, stop things and change the shape of objects. They should explore floating and sinking and relate their experiences to water safety.

Scottish 5 - 14 Curriculum: Environmental studies	
Attainment outcome	Strand
Science in the environment	Forces; Energy.
Living with technology	Technology and needs; Technology, design and control.
Investigating	Finding out; Recording; Interpreting; Reporting.
Designing and making	Planning; Making; Evaluating; Presenting.

Scottish 5 - 14 Curriculum: Mathematics			
Attainment outcome	Strand	Target	Level
Number, money, measure	Measure	Measure in easily handled standard units.	B
		Use the abbreviations m and cm, kg and g.	
		Read scales on measuring devices to the nearest graduation.	
Information handling	Collect	By obtaining information for a task.	B

▲ Name _____

Push or pull?

You will need: scissors.

▲ We can make things work or move by pushing or pulling them.

▲ Sort these objects into two groups – those you push to make them work and those you pull.

▲ Find pictures of other things which you need to push or pull to make them work.

▲ ESSENTIALS FOR SCIENCE: Pushing and pulling

▲ Name _____

Pushes and pulls in the classroom

▲ Look around your classroom. Find things that you have to push or pull to make them work or move.

▲ Draw or write down the objects you find.

Objects we **push:**

Objects we **pull:**

▲ ESSENTIALS FOR SCIENCE: Pushing and pulling

▲ Name _____

Changing shapes

▲ We can change the shapes of some objects.

▲ Look at the objects below.

▲ Draw or write down how you could change the shape of each object.

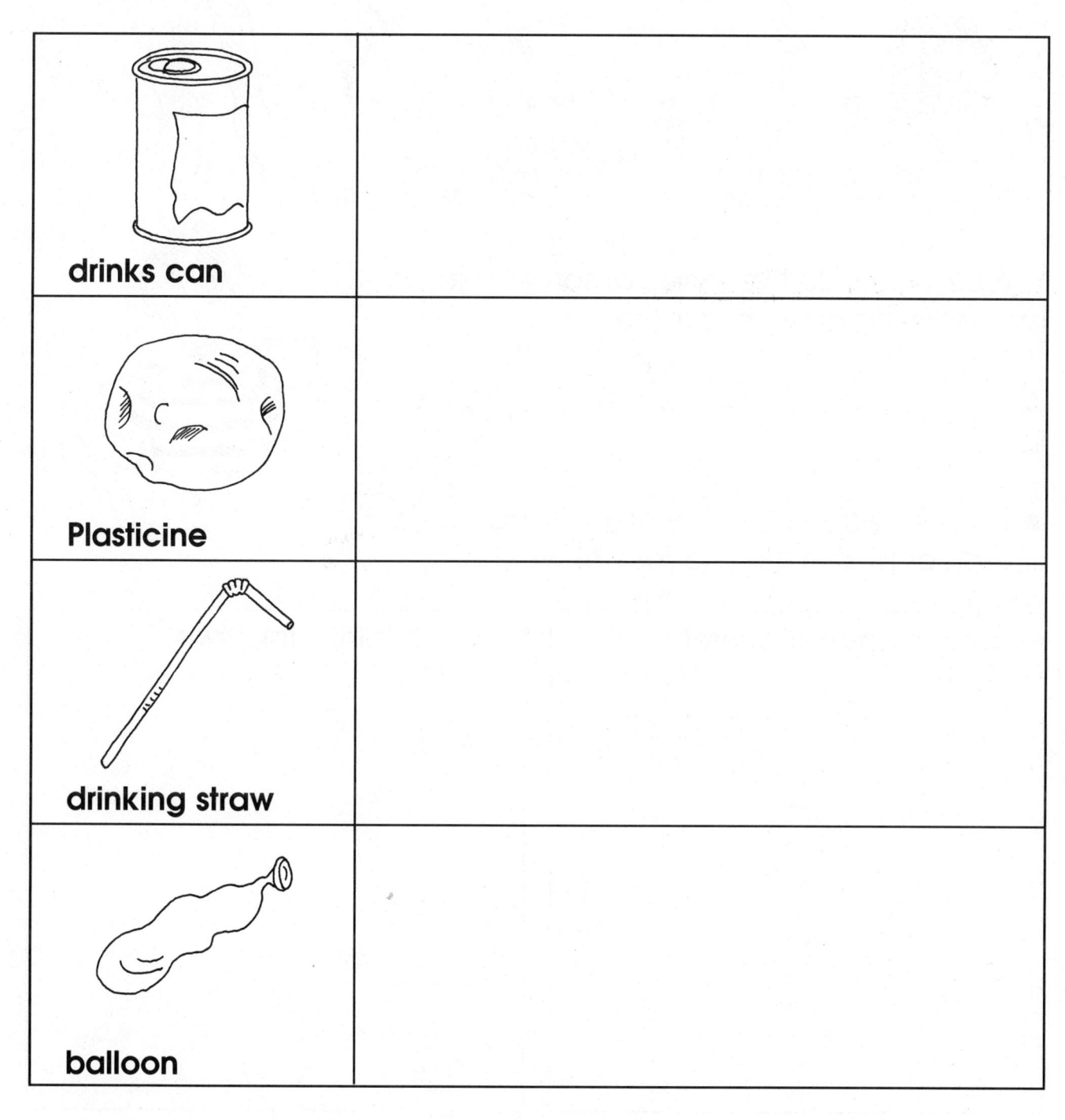

drinks can	
Plasticine	
drinking straw	
balloon	

▲ Make a collection of other objects that can change shape.

▲ ESSENTIALS FOR SCIENCE: Pushing and pulling

▲ Name _____

Stretch and twist

You will need: the objects shown below.

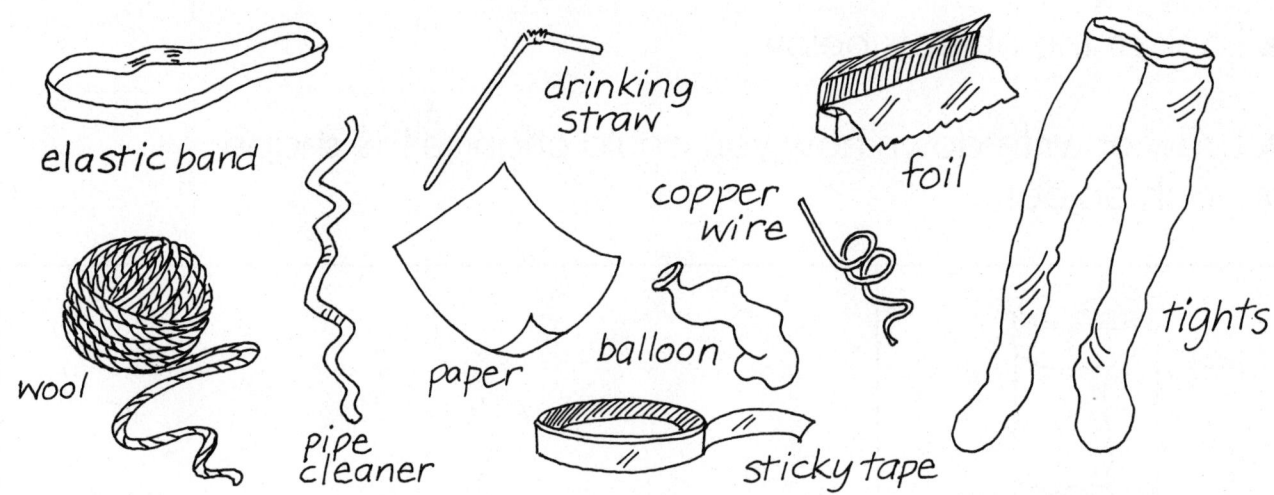

- elastic band
- wool
- pipe cleaner
- drinking straw
- paper
- copper wire
- balloon
- foil
- sticky tape
- tights

You can change the shape of some objects by stretching or twisting them.

▲ Try to stretch and twist each of the objects listed above.

▲ Draw or write down the objects that can stretch or twist in the spaces below.

Things that **stretch:**	Things that **twist:**

▲ Investigate whether other objects can be stretched or twisted.

▲ ESSENTIALS FOR SCIENCE: Pushing and pulling

▲ Name _____

Moving things

▲ **You will need:** a heavy book; string; round pencils; a piece of cloth.

▲ Place the cloth on the floor.
  • Try to push the book over it.
  • How easy is it to move?

▲ Place some pencils underneath the book.
  • Push the book along. (You will need to keep moving the back pencil to the front.)
  • Is the book easier to move now?

▲ Tie a long piece of string around the book.
  • Pull the book along the floor.
  • Is it easy to move?

▲ Try to push or pull other objects.
▲ Make a list of things we push to move and those we pull to move.

▲ ESSENTIALS FOR SCIENCE: Pushing and pulling

▲ Name _____

Make it move!

The objects below all have something missing that would stop them from moving.
▲ Draw the missing parts.

▲ Draw some other objects with the moving part missing. Ask a friend to draw the missing part.

▲ ESSENTIALS FOR SCIENCE: Pushing and pulling

▲ Name _____

Rolling things

▲ **You will need:** the objects shown below; a smooth floor surface.

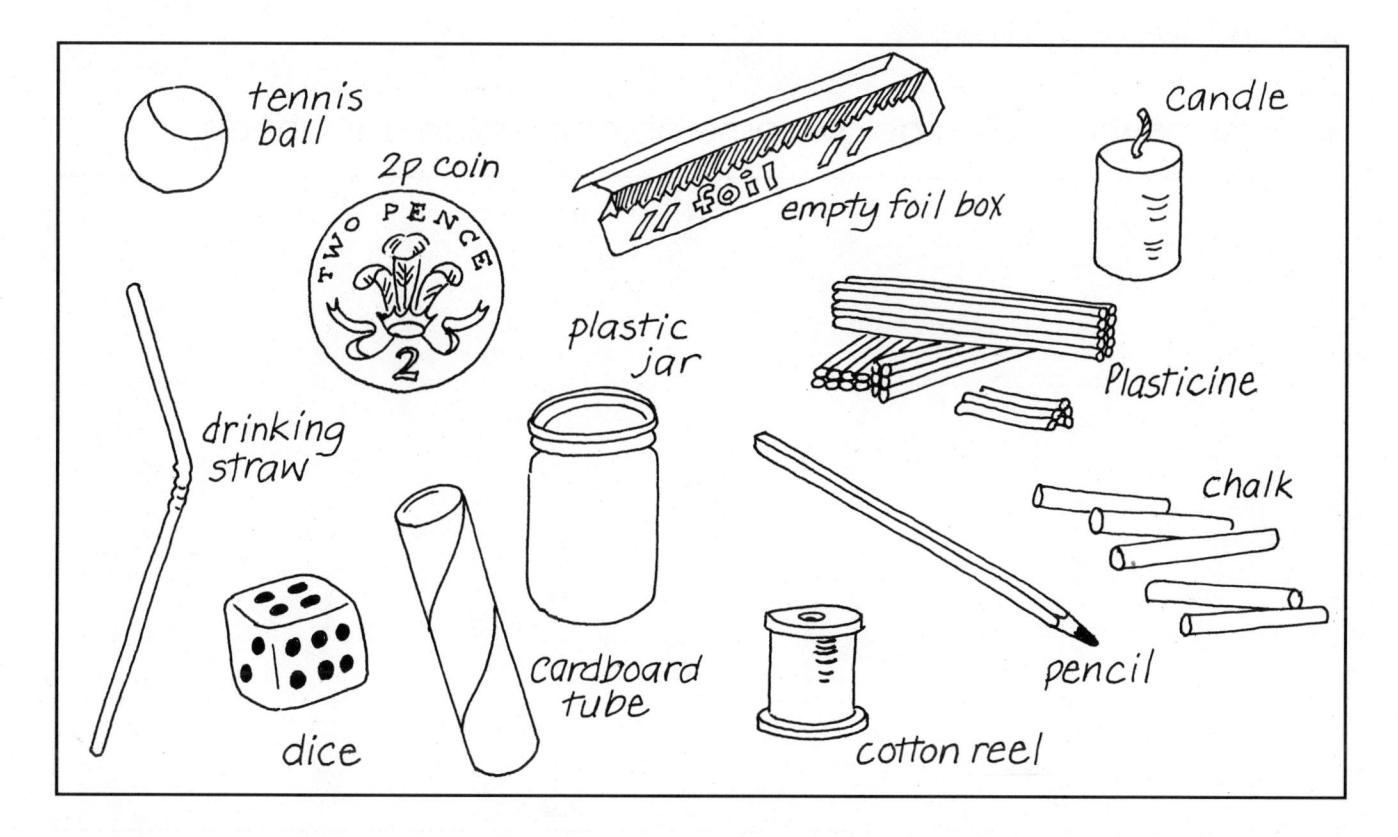

tennis ball, 2p coin, empty foil box, candle, drinking straw, plastic jar, Plasticine, chalk, dice, cardboard tube, cotton reel, pencil

▲ Roll each object along the floor.
- Which object rolls best?
- What affects how the object rolls?

Size? Shape? Weight?

▲ Try rolling some other objects. Can they all roll?

▲ ESSENTIALS FOR SCIENCE: Pushing and pulling

▲ Name _____

Wheels

You will need: dowel or cane; Plasticine; two round plastic lids (the same size); two card discs (the same size as the plastic lids).

▲ Draw or write down below some objects which use wheels.

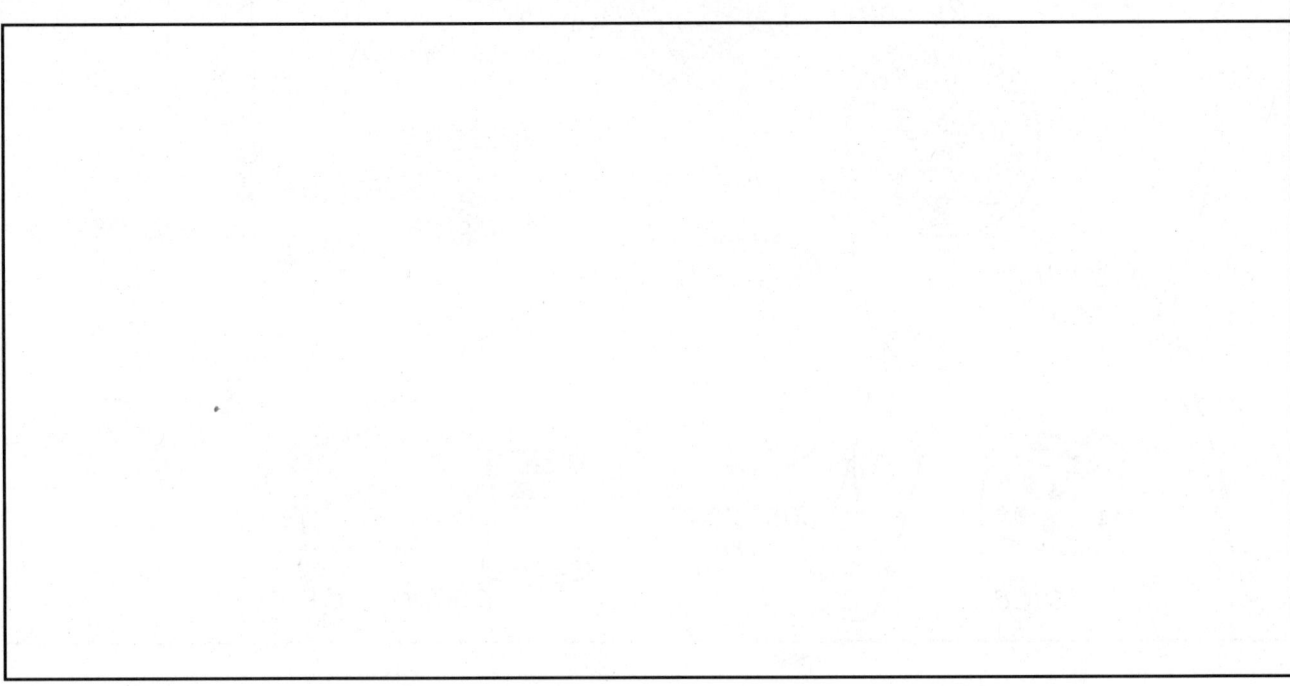

▲ Make these wheels:

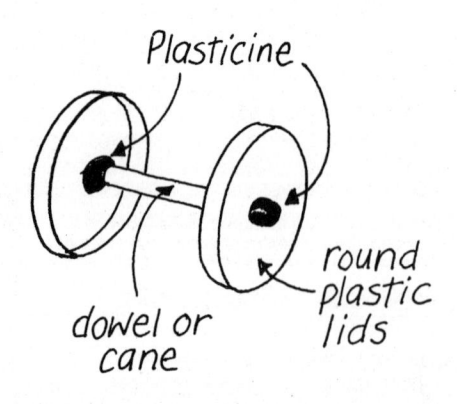

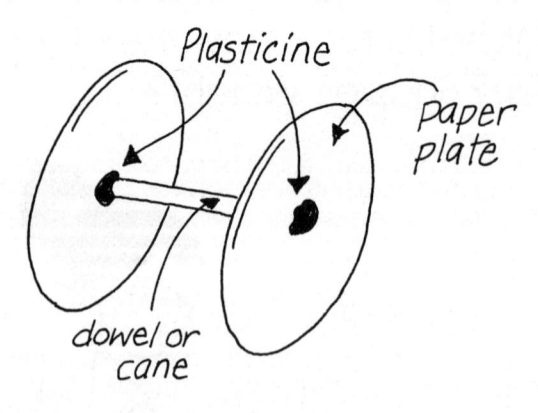

▲ Do the wheels move easily on different surfaces? Try wood, carpet, grass and tiles.
 • Is it easier to push or pull the wheels?
 • Do they move faster on a slope? Try it.

▲ Make a collection of objects which have wheels.

▲ Name _____

Make a buggy

You will need: a plastic ice-cream container; garden cane or dowelling rods; four cotton reels; drawing pins.

▲ Ask an adult to make a hole on each side of the ice-cream container large enough to push the cane rods through.

▲ Fix a cotton reel to the end of each cane and push in a drawing pin to stop the reel from coming off.

▲ Try making other types of wheels. Which ones work best?

▲ ESSENTIALS FOR SCIENCE: Pushing and pulling

▲ Name _____

Using ramps

You will need: a toy car; a length of wood or a large book; a ruler; measuring tape; books; large floor space.

▲ Place the wood on some books 10cm high so that it makes a slope. Place a toy car on the ramp and let it go.

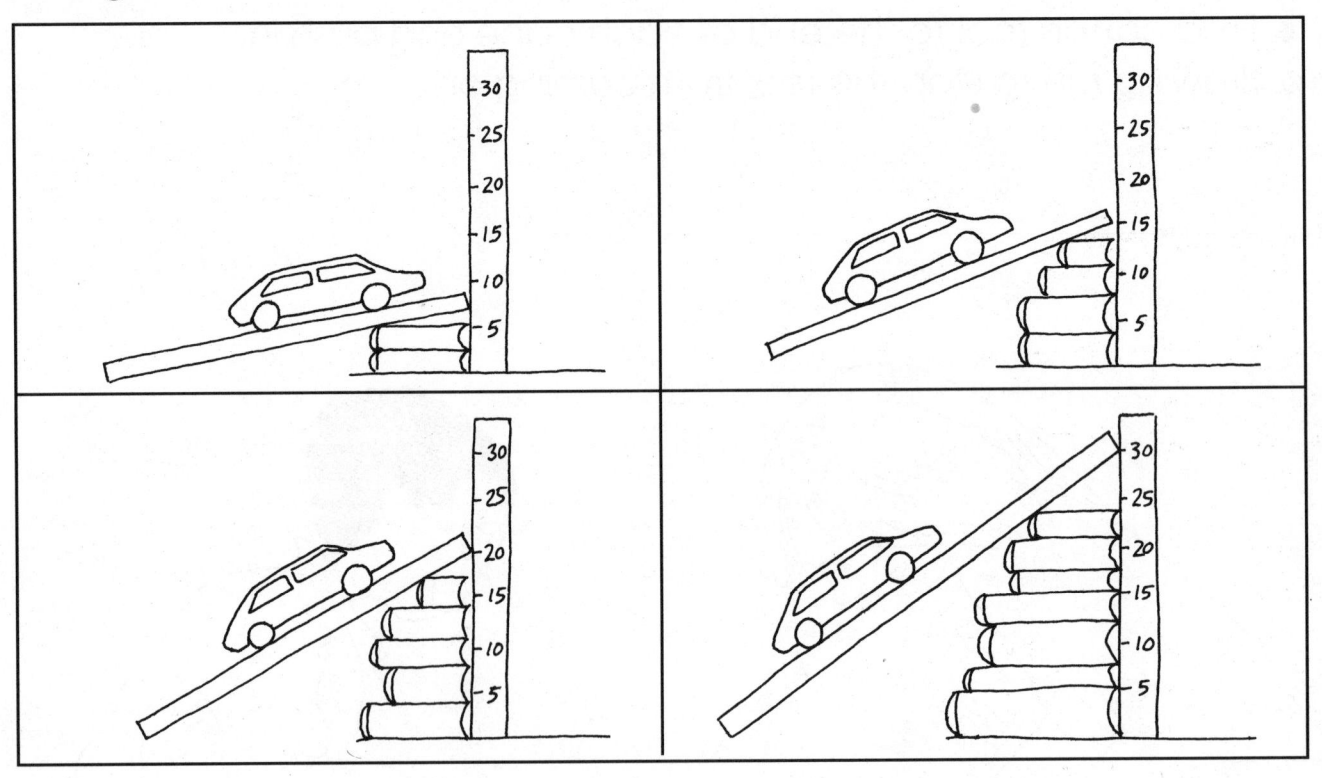

▲ Measure the distance from the end of the ramp to where the car stopped and record your results on the chart below.

Height of ramp (cm)	Distance car travelled (cm)
10 cm	
15 cm	
20 cm	
30 cm	

▲ Do the same thing with ramps 15cm, 20cm and 30cm high. What do you notice?

▲ On which ramp does the car roll furthest? Can you work out why?

▲ Try other objects on the slope. Which ones travel furthest?

▲ ESSENTIALS FOR SCIENCE: Pushing and pulling

▲ Name _____

Friction

You will need: a large book; a metal tray; a piece of wood; a piece of wood covered with fabric or sandpaper; an eraser.

▲ Lean the book against some other books so that it forms a slope.

▲ Place the eraser on the slope and watch how it moves. Does it slide freely?

▲ Keep the books in place. Try the eraser on the metal tray, the wood, the fabric or sandpaper.
- On which surface does the eraser slide best?
- Can you work out why?

▲ Discuss your results with a friend.

▲ Try out other objects on different surfaces.

▲ ESSENTIALS FOR SCIENCE: Pushing and pulling

▲ Name _____

Pendulums

You will need: Plasticine; string; a stopwatch or a watch with a second hand; two chairs or an upended desk; a ruler/measuring tape.

▲ Make two balls out of Plasticine, so that one is larger than the other. Tie some string to each ball and cut the string so that both pieces are the same length.
You have made two pendulums.

▲ Tie the pendulums to two chairs or desk legs as shown below.

▲ Time how long it takes for each pendulum to swing to and fro ten times.
  • Record your results.
  • What did you find out?

▲ Take two pieces of Plasticine of the same weight and make them into balls.
  • Try the experiment again.
  • What happens?

▲ Now use different lengths of string. What happens?

▲ Name _____

Levers – 1

You will need: an empty treacle or paint tin with the lid firmly on; a coin; a screwdriver; a hammer; a nail; a piece of wood.

▲ Try to open the tin using your fingers? Can you do this?

▲ Now try opening the tin using a coin. Is this easier? Why?

▲ Use the screwdriver to open the tin. How easy was this?

The screwdriver acts as a lever to remove the lid. It makes the lid easier to move.

▲ Hammer the nail into the piece of wood, so that half of the nail is still above the wood.

▲ Can you remove the nail with your fingers?

▲ Now use the claw hammer. Why is the hammer easier to use than your fingers?

▲ Make a list of objects that use levers, for example scissors.

▲ ESSENTIALS FOR SCIENCE: Pushing and pulling

▲ Name _____

Levers – 2

You will need: a ruler; a pencil (with flat sides); a 2p coin.

▲ Place the pencil near the edge of the table.

▲ Place the middle of the ruler on top of the pencil.

▲ Put the coin on the ruler near the pencil.

▲ Hit the ruler hard on the end that is off the table. What happens to the coin?

▲ Now move the coin further away from the pencil.
- Hit the ruler again.
- What happens to the coin?
- Has it jumped higher?

▲ Keep moving the coin along until it is at the end of the ruler. Does the coin jump higher each time?

▲ Now move the pencil closer to one end of the ruler and repeat the experiment.
- Does the coin jump higher?
- Can you suggest why?

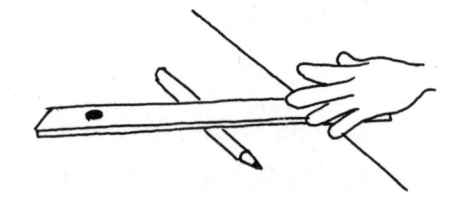

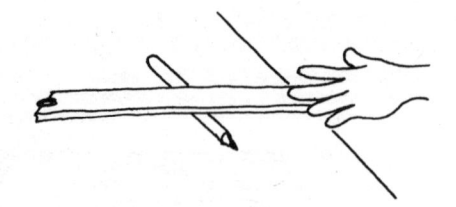

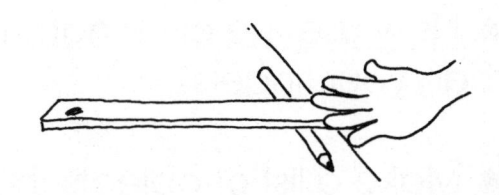

▲ ESSENTIALS FOR SCIENCE: Pushing and pulling

▲ Name _____

See-saw

You will need: a ruler; 2p coins; a pencil (with flat sides).

▲ Place the ruler on the pencil so that it balances. The pencil acts as a pivot (fulcrum).

▲ Place a 2p coin on each end of the ruler until it balances again.

▲ Add another coin to one end. What happens?

▲ Can you now make the ruler balance without adding another coin?

▲ Find out other ways to make the see-saw balance.

▲ Name _____

Make a puppet

You will need: string; paper fasteners; card; scissors; sticky tape; ice lolly stick or dowel.

This puppet uses levers to make it work.

▲ Colour the puppet and cut out the shapes.

▲ Glue the shapes on to card and cut them out.

▲ Join the arms and legs with paper fasteners.

▲ Attach the ice lolly stick to the back using sticky tape.

▲ Join the string to the paper fasteners as shown below.

▲ Design and make another puppet.

▲ ESSENTIALS FOR SCIENCE: Pushing and pulling

▲ Name _____

Lifting things

You will need: a string or thin rope; a cotton reel; a small plastic bucket; heavy objects such as toy bricks; wire; a hook placed at child height.

▲ Fill the bucket with heavy objects.

▲ Lift the bucket with one hand. How difficult is it to move?

▲ Now use both hands. Is this easier?

▲ Make a triangle from wire and attach a cotton reel.

▲ Hang the wire from a hook.

▲ Tie the string to the bucket.

▲ Wind the string over the cotton reel. You have made a pulley.

▲ Pull on the string to lift the bucket.
  • Is it easier to lift the bucket now?
  • Can you make it easier using more cotton reels?

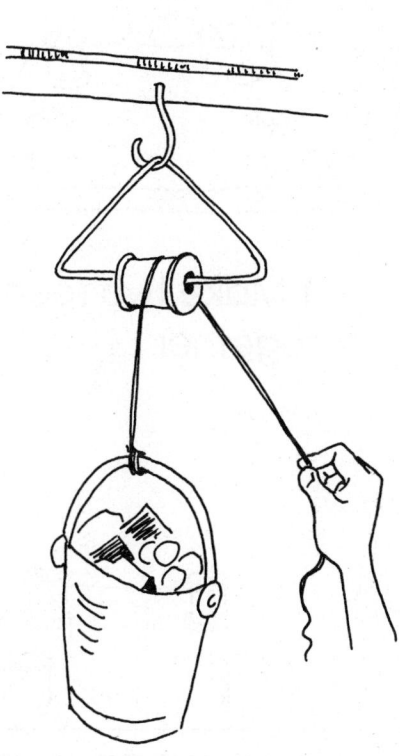

▲ ESSENTIALS FOR SCIENCE: Pushing and pulling

▲ Name _____

Making things turn

You will need: a piece of wood; four large nails; four cotton reels; a hammer; two strong elastic bands.

▲ Hammer a nail into each corner of the piece of wood. Sit a cotton reel over each nail.

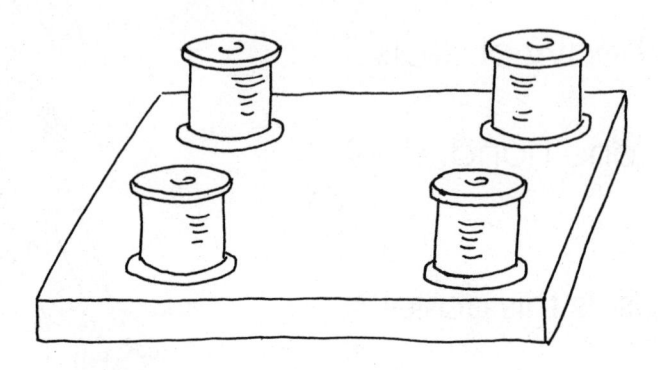

▲ Use the elastic bands to make the reels turn in the ways shown below. Draw on the pictures where you placed the elastic bands.

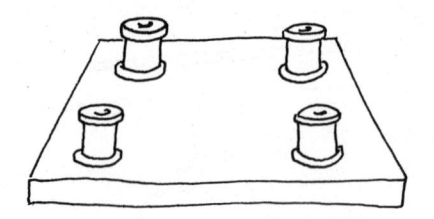

1 Make two reels turn together.

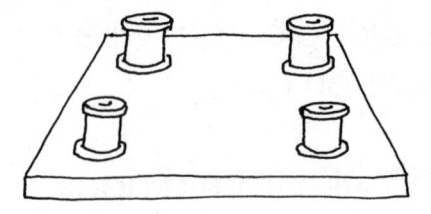

2 Make diagonally opposite reels turn together.

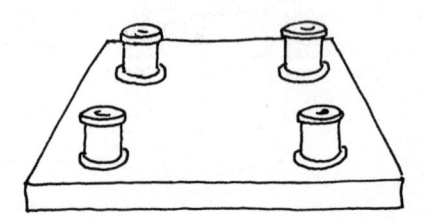

3 Make three reels turn together.

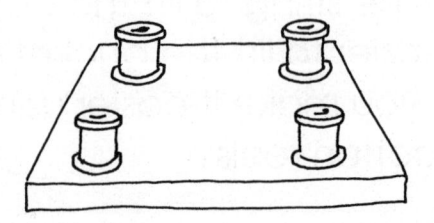

4 Make four reels turn together.

▲ ESSENTIALS FOR SCIENCE: Pushing and pulling

▲ Name _____

Cogs and gears

You will need: round boxes (cheese boxes) of different sizes; corrugated cardboard; nails; a hammer; a piece of wood; glue.

▲ Cut out strips of corrugated card to the same width as the edge of the cheese boxes. Glue the card round the edges of the boxes as shown.

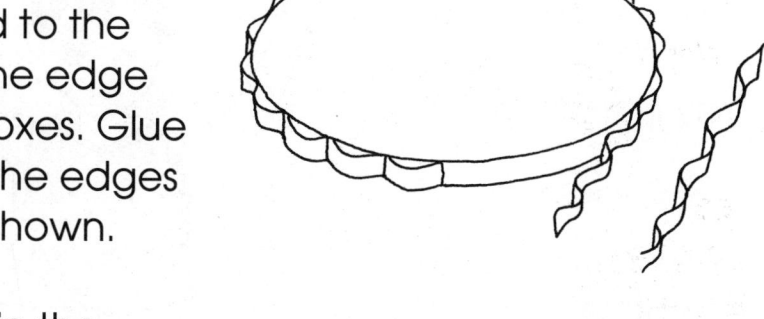

▲ Pierce a hole in the centre of each box and nail them to the piece of wood so that the teeth of each wheel meet each other.

▲ Make a hole in one wheel near the edge and use a nail as a handle to turn the wheels.

▲ Mark each wheel where the teeth meet.

▲ Make the big wheel turn once.
  • How many times did the medium wheel turn?
  • How many times did the small wheel turn?
  • Which wheel turns more quickly?
  • Do the wheels turn in the same direction?

▲ What kinds of things use cogs and gears? Make a list of them.

▲ ESSENTIALS FOR SCIENCE: Pushing and pulling

▲ Name _____

How things fall

You will need: two objects of the same shape and size but different weights, such as a sponge ball and a tennis ball or a golf ball and a ping-pong ball; two sheets of paper the same size; a tin tray.

▲ Place the tray in front of a chair.

▲ Stand on the chair and hold the objects up as high as you can at the same level.

▲ Let go of them at the same time.
  • Which one do you think will hit the tray first?
  • Do you hear them land together?

▲ Try out other objects of the same size and shape but different weights. What happens?

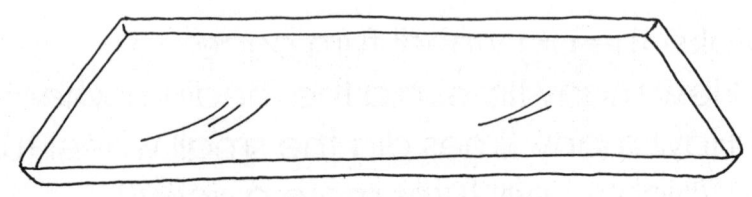

▲ Now screw up one of the sheets of paper into a ball. Leave the other sheet flat. Drop these together.
  • What happens?
  • Can you work out why?

▲ ESSENTIALS FOR SCIENCE: Pushing and pulling

▲ Name _____

How hard does it fall?

You will need: soft modelling clay; a ball of Plasticine; a ruler; a metre stick.

▲ Make the clay into a thick, flat shape and place it on the floor.

▲ Drop the ball of Plasticine on to the clay from different heights and measure the size of the hole that the Plasticine makes in the clay.

▲ Record your results below:

Height Plasticine dropped from	Size of hole left in clay
15cm	
30cm	
60cm	
1 metre	
2 metres	

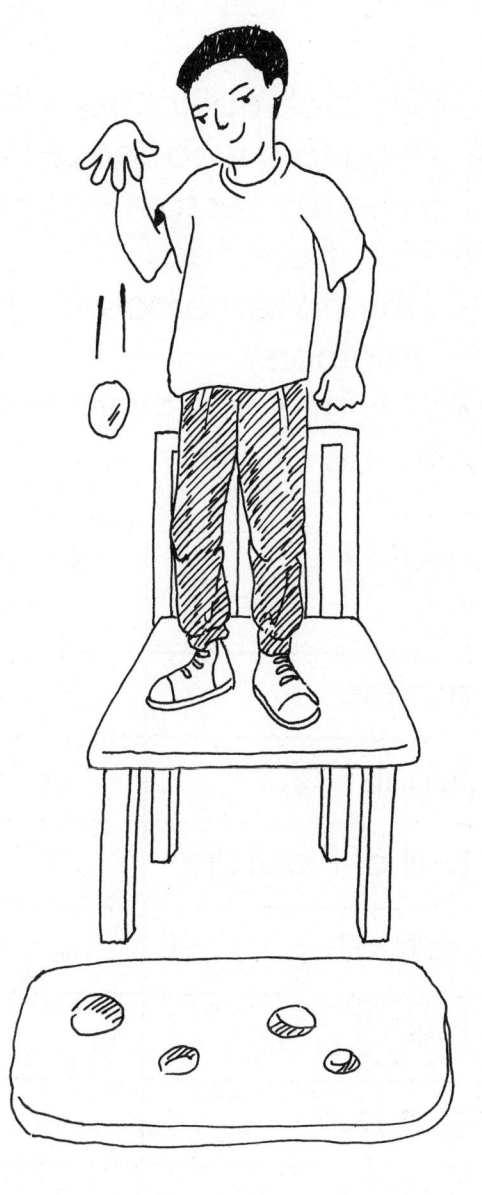

▲ What happens to the size of the hole as you drop the Plasticine from greater heights? Why do you think this happens?

▲ Drop other objects on to the clay. Do harder objects make bigger dents?

▲ ESSENTIALS FOR SCIENCE: Pushing and pulling

▲ Name _____

Will it bounce?

You will need: a metre ruler or measuring tape fixed to the wall; the objects listed below. Work with a friend.

▲ Look at the list of objects below.

▲ Predict which objects will bounce.

▲ Drop each object from the same height on to a wooden or tiled floor. Use a metre ruler to measure how high they bounced.
  • Why do some bounce better than others?
  • Why do some things not bounce at all?

Object	Prediction: will it bounce?	Result: how high did it bounce?
marble		
tennis ball		
ball of Plasticine		
netball		
ball of paper		
golf ball		
cricket ball		
dice		
ping-pong ball		

▲ Try out some more objects.

▲ ESSENTIALS FOR SCIENCE: Pushing and pulling

▲ Name _____

Sink or float?

You will need: a bowl or bucket of water; the objects listed below.

▲ Look at the objects listed below.

▲ Predict whether you think each object will float or sink.

▲ Test each one to see if you were right.

Object	Prediction: will it sink or float?	Result: did it sink or float?
paper-clip		
marble		
bean seed		
plastic ruler		
wood		
spoon		
glass jar		
wooden peg		
foil tray		

▲ Now try out other objects.

▲ ESSENTIALS FOR SCIENCE: Pushing and pulling

▲ Name _____

Does shape affect floating?

You will need: a bowl or bucket of water; Plasticine.

▲ Make the Plasticine into the shapes shown below.
▲ Put each shape in the water. What happens?

Shape		Result : sink or float?
○	ball shape	
⬭	sausage shape	
▭	flat shape	
◻	cube shape	

▲ Now make a boat from the Plasticine.
▲ Draw the boat you made in the space below.
Did it float?

▲ Experiment with different boat shapes. Draw them and say whether they sank or floated.

▲ How does shape affect whether it sinks or floats?

▲ ESSENTIALS FOR SCIENCE: Pushing and pulling   28

▲ Name _____

Feeling the 'push' of water

You will need: a ping-pong ball; a jar or tank of water; various weights 1g–50g; sticky tape; masking/coloured tape.

▲ Put some water in the tank. Mark the water level with masking tape on the outside of the container.

▲ Put the ball in the water. What happens?

▲ Now push down on the ball with your hand. Try to make the ball sink.
 • What can you feel?
 • What happens to the water level when your hand goes into the water?
 • Why does this happen?

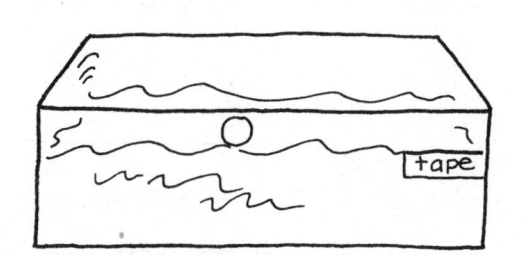

▲ Now attach weights to the ball and try to make it sink.
 • Predict the result before you try each weight.
 • Say what happens.

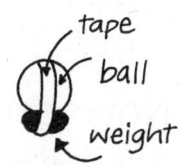

Weight	Prediction: will it sink?	Result: did it sink?	Water level: what happened?
1g			
5g			
10g			
20g			
50g			

▲ ESSENTIALS FOR SCIENCE: Pushing and pulling

▲ Name _____

Is salty water best for floating?

You will need: Plasticine; plastic counters or cubes; a container of water (with clear sides); salt.

▲ Make a boat shape from the Plasticine.
  • Make sure it will float in the container of water.
  • Is it floating high or low in the water?

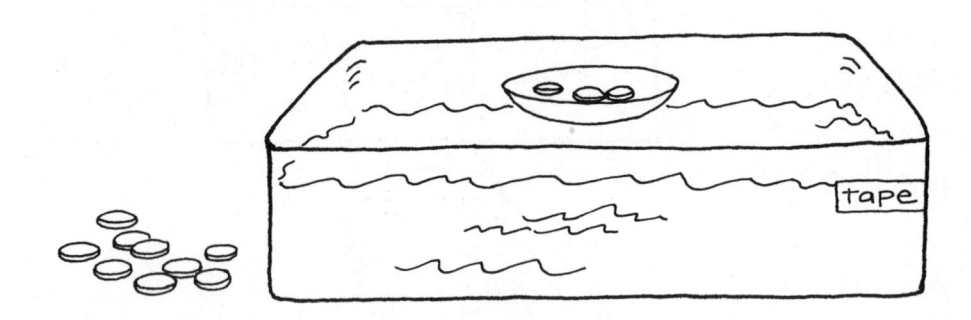

▲ Now add counters one at a time into the boat.
• Count how many counters it takes to sink the boat.
• Write your answer below:

   It took ☐ counters to sink my boat.

▲ Now take the boat out of the water and dissolve lots of salt in the water.

▲ Put your boat in the water and do the experiment again. By now the boat will have absorbed some water and become heavier. Write your result below:

   It took ☐ counters to sink my boat in salty water.

▲ Can you explain the result?

▲ Try other liquids such as cooking oil, milk or soft drinks. How well does the boat float?

▲ ESSENTIALS FOR SCIENCE: Pushing and pulling

▲ Name _____

Water safety

▲ Imagine that your friend has fallen into a swimming pool and cannot swim.

There are some objects nearby which you could throw in to help your friend to float in the water until help arrives.

▲ Put a tick next to any object below that would float if you threw it in to the water.

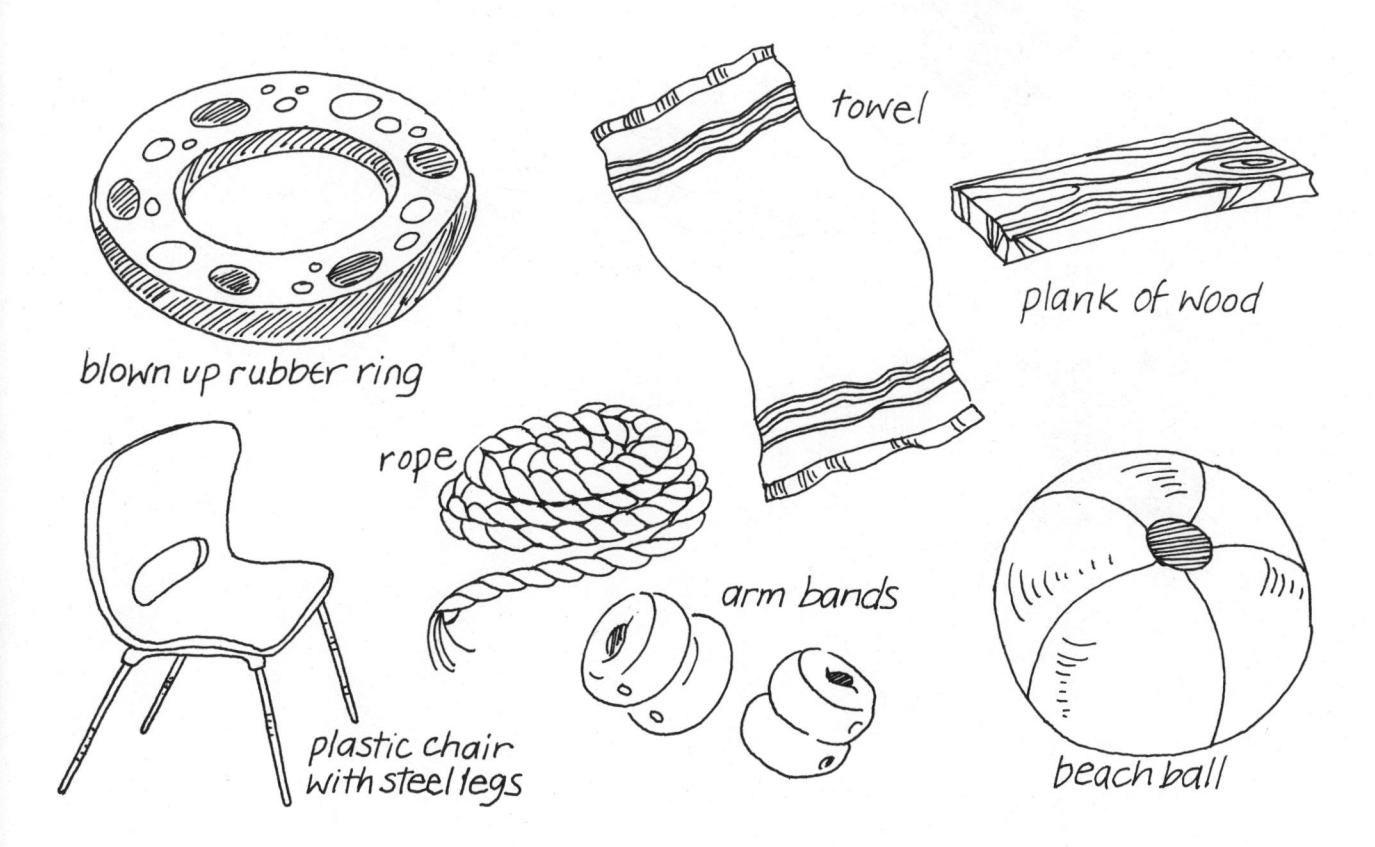

blown up rubber ring

towel

plank of wood

plastic chair with steel legs

rope

arm bands

beach ball

▲ ESSENTIALS FOR SCIENCE: Pushing and pulling

▲ Name _____

Balloon power

You will need: a piece of wood; a balloon; a small piece of plastic tube; a round bracket; nails or screws.

▲ Make a flat boat shape from the wood.

▲ Insert the piece of plastic tube into the neck of the balloon. Tape the bracket to the top of the boat over the neck of balloon.

▲ Blow up the balloon and let the boat go on the water. What causes the boat to move?